Down t

Poems About Life

*Best Wishes Mick
from
Duggy*

By

Duggy Verrill

Published by Duggy Verrill

Copyright - © 2011 Duggy Verrill

Cover Photograph by Paul Bittlestone

The right of Duggy Verrill to be identified as the author of this work has been asserted by him in accordance with the Copyright, Designs and Patents Act 1988

First published in 2011 by
Duggy Verrill

Apart from any use permitted under UK copyright law this publication may only be reproduced, stored or transmitted, in any form, or by any means, with prior permission in writing of the publisher, or in the case of reprographic production, in accordance with the terms of licences issue by the Copyright Licensing Agency.

All characters in this publication are fictitious and any resemblance to real persons, living or dead, is purely coincidental.

To everyone who lived in Albany Street, Middlesbrough in the 60's. We had 'nowt' but looking back we had everything. Special thanks to my Dad Roly for those drawings.

MEMORY LANE

Looking in the mirror lately
I'm feeling something's missing
I seem to spend most of my time
Just sat here reminiscing

I've lived in Middlesbrough all my life
There's loads of things I miss
So if you got five minutes to spare
Let's just reminisce

Summer afternoons in Albert Park
Picnics in the shade
Jam sandwiches from the golly-wog jar
Lowcocks Lemonade

A ride on the Miniature Railway
Choking on the smoke
Half an hour on the skating rink
Three straws in a bottle of Coke

A Knickerbocker Glory in Rea's Café
Juke-box playing our favourite track
Parkers Grill for breakfast
With fish tanks out the back

Buying toys from Nelsons
Or Romer Parish's Shop
Records from Alan Fearnley's
Or food from the Co-op

You could always use the Provi
Or get an Uptons Card
H.P. was always available
Good job, 'cos times were hard

Parker Coats from Work-Wear
Also Monkey Boots
For weddings or for funerals
Burton's had your suits

The General Hospital for broken bones
No computers or mobile phones
The Infirmary; Ear, Nose and Throat
Milkmen driving round on floats

Summer nights at Gilkes Street Baths
All best friends and having laughs
Then a bag of chips at the Little Chef
If we had any money left

Trying for strikes at the Bowling Alley
On top of Frankie Dees
Sunday afternoons in the Clarence Club
Watching ladies do striptease

Young lads getting tattooed
Sinbad's was the best
'Love' and 'Hate' on your knuckles
Or a dancing girl on your chest

Saturday morning at the cinema
The Odeon or the A.B.C.
The one who paid opened the fire door
Then we'd all get in for free

Saturday dinners was Upex Pies
North Ormesby Road the place
The very best pies in Middlesbrough
And gravy all over your face

Saturday afternoons at Ayresome Park
I loved that Holgate roar
It was worth the shilling to get in
Just to see John Hickton score

On Saturday night was The Raglan
The Shaky, Masham then The Grand
And grab a sausage going down
Off the bloke on the hot-dog stand

We'd finish up at the Claggy Mat
We had some smashing nights
If you were getting nowhere with the lasses
You could stand and watch the fights

Then into the Boro Fish Bar
Cod and chips were still quite cheap
Their stuff tasted lovely
If your taste buds had gone to sleep

Hope you've enjoyed going down memory lane
Maybe in 30 years we'll do it again
All of us have got a story
Thanks for listening, to Jackanory.

ME DAD

Putting me Dad in the care home today
It's not such a wrench 'cos he's been getting in the way
He's starting to smell and there's a stain on his pants
Most of the time he just sits in a trance

His eating habits are a little bit much
Porridge starts in his mouth and ends upon his crotch
He chokes on his soup it goes all up the walls
He's just an embarrassment if anyone calls

It wouldn't be so bad if he could make it to the loo
But many a time he says, "Son, I've followed through"
He says it with sadness and a tear in his eye
He says to me, "Son, I wish I could die"

"I've got it all up me arm and under me nail"
It's all up his goolies and all up his tail
It's not that he's worried, it's happened before
The only thing is that was when he was four

You did all these things for me when I was a kid
I'll always remember the things that you did
You always loved me and spoiled me rotten
The least I can do, Dad, is wipe your bottom

I said, "Matron, here's me Dad, look after him well"
These last couple of weeks with him have been hell
It's not that we don't love him, we'd keep him till the end
It's just his bloody whinging is driving us round the bend

BITTER

When you first fall in love
You say 'Thanks' to the Lord above
He sent you the perfect mate
And you got everything, worth the wait

Beautiful eyes, luscious lips
Shapely breasts, sexy hips
Proud to have her on your arm
So hot she'd set off a smoke alarm

Catchin' lads gawp and stare
Thinking what they'd do to her
Posh restaurant, expensive meals
Suspenders and stiletto heals

But as the years slowly pass
Droopy breasts and big fat ass
Where's that sexy little chick
You're with the wife, she makes you sick

Hairs gone grey, wrinkly face
Figure only a dog would chase
Got the smell of stilton cheese
Plastic hip and knobbly knees

Regret the day I tied the knot
Took me for everything I got
Got the house, the car, divorce
Expensive thing this intercourse!

ALBERT PARK

Dropped me car off in the village
It was due for its test
Took the afternoon off work
Thought I'd 'ave a few hours rest

It was a sunny September afternoon
The sun was very low
I thought I'd spend an hour in Albert Park
And remember where we used to go

I sat down on the first bench
A smart young lady was reading a book
I smiled, she gave me a nasty stare
She said, "Piss off perve and sling yer hook"

I said, "I haven't opened me mouth"
She said, "That's before you do"
"It's not safe for a woman like me
When there's blokes about like you"

I thought I'd better make a move
I said, "Thank you for the chat"
She said, "Don't be sarcastic
Sod off you sad old twat"

I strolled towards the fountain
Two Rotties were off the lead
After meeting Hitler's daughter
This is something I don't need

One came pounding at me
The bloke said, "Just stand still"
Seeing as my legs had gone
I thought, I think I will

Have you ever tried standing still
When you're shaking like a leaf
All I could see coming at me
Was a set of Rotties teeth

The Rottie stopped right in front of me
The bloke said, "It could smell your fear"
If it had come a little closer mate
It might have smelt some diarrhoea

Some lads were drinking Cider
Down beside the skating rink
I said, "'Ave you got a spare one lads?"
"I wouldn't mind a drink"

I was only being friendly
I didn't want no grief
One said, "Would your lass recognise you mate,
If you went home with no teeth?"

I thought I'd better leave the park
While I'm still in one piece
I think the people I've met in here
Are just on day release

I hope my car has passed its test
I pray it doesn't fail
I'd have had a friendlier afternoon
If I'd 'ave been in Home House Gaol.

Albert Park, a lovely place
A cheery smile, a friendly face
Maybe 30 years ago
But today, I don't think so.

PRIVATE THOUGHTS OF THE VICAR

The Christening

Baptising Mick and Carol's baby today, the bloody stuck up pair
He looks like a woman with his dyed blond curly hair
She's in charge, with beady eyes and a smile that makes me sick
He looks more like Carol and she looks more like Mick
What an ugly baby, no surprise though, what a shame
If he knew about his parents he'd crawl back from where he came.

The Wedding

I'm marrying Steve and Jill today, an uglier pair you'll never see
I've looked at her a few times and thought "rather him than me"
I'm sure when they've said "I do" they'll wish they'd said "I don't"
And when they undress on their wedding night I'm sure they'll say "I won't"

The Funeral

I'm burying Agnes Smith today she was 86 years old
A dirtier woman you'd never meet, I'm sure she was covered in mould
Whenever she came near me, the smell, it made me sick
I'd say, "I'm in a hurry Aggie, you'll have to make it quick"
Thank Goodness she'll be underground in just a couple of hours
Please donate to Children in Need, 'cos her smell could kill the flowers.

MOTHER-IN-LAW

It's that time of year again
Mother-in-Law comes to stay
She's losing her memory
But she always remembers the way

She thinks I've got a soft spot for her
I've got a few of them
My favourite one's up Acklam Road
A plot in the local crem'

She rabbits on for hours and hours
The wife just disappears
I try my best to look interested
The old goat bores me to tears

She talks about 'the olden days'
She misses her husband Jim
I always try to cheer her up
Saying, "You'll soon be buried next to him"

I try to be nice for the week
I take her breakfast and papers in bed
Some mornings in her bedroom
She smells as tho' she's dead

She's always welcome in our house
This year she looks quite ill
She's really cheered me up this time
I'm looked after in her will

The taxi's here, she's going home
The smell of her just lingers
I always like to wave her off
I only use two fingers

MICK

I've lost me whippet Mick
Mick was the love of me life
If ever the truth was told
I loved him more than I love the wife

I'd had him since a puppy
Since that day our love just grew
If Mick had ever learned how to talk
He'd say, "Duggy I love you"

We'd sit and watch the telly
Cuddled up on the settee
I'd sit and stroke his head
Mick meant the world to me

He had the best of everything
Chicken and brazing steak,
I'd sit with a paste sandwich
And finish off with a fatty cake

When I took him round the town
The kids would come and shout, "There's Mick"
He got patted so much some days
I'm sure that Mick got sick

We'd go everywhere together
Morning, noon and night
If Mick was not beside me
It just didn't seem quite right

I had him off the lead one morning
Something spooked poor Mick
He disappeared around the corner
I didn't know he could run that quick

I heard a car's brakes screech
And then a horrible sound
I rushed around the bend
Mick was on the ground

I could see him underneath the car
I just sat there full of grief
His body wasn't moving
There was blood and snot and teeth

My friend said , 'Duggy just look away
I can see how hurt you are"
The bloke who had been driving
Said, "He's scratched me bloody car!"

Me mate said, "I will sort this out
You make your way back home"
Mick wasn't beside me now
I felt so all alone

Me mate called with a glass case
"It's Mick I've had him stuffed"
It didn't quite look like him
But he could see that I was chuffed

I've got him in the corner now
He's groomed and nicely washed
Me mate put a different head on him
'Cos the other one got squashed.

BULLIED

Is it 'cos I've got ginger hair?
And freckles on me face?
Is it 'cos I'm covered in spots?
I also wear a brace

Is it 'cos I'm fat?
Or is it 'cos I'm thin?
Is it 'cos I wear trendy clothes?
Or clothes that you'd put in the bin?

Is it 'cos me eye's not straight?
Is it 'cos I've got big ears?
Or is it that they know I'm easy
To have in floods of tears?

Is it 'cos I'm little?
Or is it 'cos I'm tall?
Could it be that they've found out
I've only got one ball?

Is it 'cos I'm black?
Or is it 'cos I'm white?
Is it 'cos I'm quiet
And I don't put up a fight?

Is it 'cos my teeth are buck
And they all think it's funny?
When I'm walking down the corridor
I hear 'em shouting, "Here's Bugs Bunny"

Why do they spit at me?
I know spit doesn't hurt
But it's not nice sat in lessons
With greenies on your shirt

Is it 'cos me Mam and Dad
Struggle to get by?
Or is it 'cos Dad's loaded
And I'm learning how to fly?

Is it 'cos we shop at Netto
And the kids all think we're skint?
Is it 'cos we shop at Waitrose
And they think we're worth a mint?

A bully is a bully who can ruin someone's life
They could end up as someone's husband,
Or maybe someone's wife

They might have their own children
I'd like to wish them well
Hope they don't end up like Mam or Dad
And make other kid's lives hell.

ME WHITE BIRTHDAY SUIT

Me 60th Birthday on Saturday
Gonna have a night down town
Just treated meself to a spray tan
I'm a lovely golden brown

Just bought meself a white suit
And a beautiful white shirt
Watch out all you ladies
Someone's gonna get hurt!

I've left me top buttons open
You can see me hairy chest
I've got me gold medallion on
And binned me white string vest

I've started in 'The Alice'
There was a band just going on
One lad shouted, "Oi mate,
Where's Olivia Newton-John?"

He looked a handy geezer
I just had a little smirk
His friend said, "You look like the dead one
Out of Randall and Hopkirk"

Next I went over to Yates's
Three young 'crackers' were out for a drink
I thought just go and order your pint
Sip it slowly and maybe throw them a wink

I said "Can I join you ladies?"
"It's me Birthday and I'm out on my own"
One said, "Won't they be worried about you?"
I said, "Who?" she said "The care home"

I laughed and said, "You cheeky mare,
I've just come over for a little chat"
She said, "I hope that's all you've come for
'Cos you'll get nothing more than that"

I thought I'd go out for a fag
And take in some fresh air
I was getting nowhere fast
With the Beverly Sisters in there

I thought I'd go and have a couple,
Over in 'The Oak'
I'd only been in two minutes
When I got chatted up by a bloke

I smiled at him and said, "Alright mate
I'm not that way inclined"
He said, "Well what a pity,
You've got a beautiful behind"

I jokingly said, "You can have me
But only in your dreams"
His mate shouted over, "If your van's outside
Would you bring us two ice-creams!"

I finished off me drink
Went over to the taxi rank
Things weren't going as I had planned
If I'm to be totally frank

I said to the driver, "Park Hotel mate"
He said, "You're dressed up, are you going on a date?"
"No just one more pint I'm chilled to the bones"
"When you were walking to the taxi I thought you were Tom Jones!"

I walked into the bar and ordered a beer
Some smart arse shouted, "The Seafood bloke's here!"
I must be honest I've had the shits of a night
Come me next birthday I'm not gonna wear white.

MACKERAL BASHING

Enjoy your day at South Gare
Smell of murder in the air
A peaceful man when he's at home
But not when he's in the 'killing zone'

Sticks with twine and jagged hooks
Catchin' fish that no-one cooks
Weathered faces burnt and red
Not happy til the Macky's dead

Tugged in on the end of line
Sometimes 3 or 4 a time
Glistening silver, fighting, flappin'
Excited killers, whistling, clappin'

Smash their heads against the floor
Still not dead give him some more
Spurting blood from mouth and gills
Hope these fish have written their wills

Quick throw in another line
Take the bait, I hope it's mine
Reeks of death how cruel we are
An open air abattoir

Hope these men don't buy a gun
Time for us to learn to run
Picks us off and then re-load
I think I'll stop using the Trunk Road

THE WIFE

Met the wife 30 years ago when we were both seventeen
I was the luckiest lad in Middlesbrough
I'd bagged the local Beauty Queen

She had a size 10 figure on the day that we first met
But ever since that time
All she seems to have done is 'ett'

She doesn't seem to notice, every day she's getting bigger
When I comment on how nice she looks
She says, "I like to watch my figure"

Her size doesn't bother me, every day I love her more
But when she's trying clothes on
Now she's up to a 34!

When I watch her do the shopping I worry about me cash
She goes at 50 miles an hour
It's like she's won the trolley dash

After we'd finished shopping I said, "Would you like a bite to eat?"
She said, "I wouldn't mind Darl',
And take the weight of me feet"

I said, "I'll 'ave a teacake with me cup of tea"
She said, "I'll just have fish and chips,
Eeee yer don't half spoil me"

I said, "It's only half past 9", she said "I've had nowt
to eat at all"
She said, "I've been feeling dizzy
I know you'd hate to see me fall"

She finished off her breakfast in three minutes flat
I looked at her and said,
"My Love you really enjoyed that"

She said "Before we leave the Centre, I'll nip into the
Anne Summers store
I said, "You don't need any underwear Dear
It's full, your knickers draw"

She picked up the tiniest thong and said, "Do you like
this Dear?"
I thought if she tries to put that on
It's gonna disappear

Then she's waving a size 12 Basque at me saying,
"What do you think of this?"
I smile at her politely,
I'm sure she's taking the piss

So now we're home, the shopping's done for another
week
She's maxed out me credit card,
I'm sure I heard it squeak

I'm gonna love her all my life, she's never done me any wrong
It's getting near to bedtime now,
I hope she didn't buy that thong.

GRACE

Taking me friend down town shopping today
She's in a wheelchair so we'll get in the way
Nobody moves as I push her around
Keep out of our way or end up on the ground

We start at McDonalds she says, "It's my treat"
I said, "It's too full Love, we won't get a seat"
She said, "It's ok 'cos I've got my chair"
I'll have to stand, life's so unfair

In to WH Smith's to buy her best friend a gift
I'll use the stairs and you grab the lift
When I get to the top there's no Grace and no chair
Then she shouts from the lift, 'Is there anyone there?"

The lift engineer arrives in the hour
He says, "This won't take long you'll soon be out Flower"
"No problem" she says, "I'm not in a hurry"
She doesn't mind so why do I worry

We're back in the town in the charity shops
I'm looking at jeans she's looking at tops
My jeans are too short her top is too tight
It's hard finding something that fits us just right

We bump into Joe he asks, "Is she alright?"
I say, "Ask her yourself Joe, she's really quite bright,
Just because she's sat in the chair
Doesn't mean she isn't all there"

Joe goes all red, he's embarrassed a bit
He looks at my friend and says "I feel like a tit"
She tells him, "Don't worry, it happens all of the time
Just get on with your life like I get on with mine"

So next time you see me with my friend Grace
('Cos we tend to pop up all over the place)
Remember it's not nice if you stop and stare
'Cos come the next life it could be you in the chair.

CONFUSED

A new lad started school today
Sat next to me, I know he's gay
His mam's a teacher, dad's a banker
Got a gorgeous sister called Bianca

We're all fifteen and I'm in love
With Sandra from the year above
Find myself talking tough
So he doesn't think that I'm a poof

It's ten o'clock, time for break
Would he pull out a fairy cake?
What do gay people drink?
Would his lunchbox be bright pink?

Would he have coffee or tea?
Pull up a chair or sit on me knee?
Tell me I've got lovely eyes?
Will his hand go for me flies?

He said, "I'll get the teas"
I shouted, "two sugars please"
"Don't worry" he said, "I'll pay"
He touched my cup, could I turn gay?

Dinner time we had a scream
Dinner time I had a dream
We talked about all kinds of things
From holidays to wedding rings

I really enjoyed meself today
I never had a friend who's gay
He didn't try to kiss me or feel up my behind
I just can't understand folks with a narrow mind

SUICIDE

I'm thinking about finishing it all
I'm trying to end my life
I've got nothing in the bank
And I'm fed up with the wife

I went and bought meself a rope
It's said the good die young
And our lass always said to me
I wish you were well hung

I jumped off the table
I pulled down half the roof
I've finished up with a broken leg
And chipped me right front tooth

I lined the paracetamols up
I was feeling down the other night
I'd only taken two of them
I started to feel alright

I was gonna jump off a car park roof
I peeped over the side
I've always been scared stiff of heights
I came down, I nearly died

I bought meself a hose-pipe
Gonna gas meself in the car
It blew up, I'd put Diesel in
It should've been four star

I put my head in the oven
I thought this can't be that hard
The gas stopped after a minute
There was nowt left on the card

I've thought about slitting me wrists
But I really don't think I could
I've never been one for pain
And I hate the sight of blood

I jumped into the River Tees
A bloke spotted me in a passing lorry
He dived in and pulled me out
I was clinging to a shopping trolley

I sat on the railway line
I was sure a train was due
Stayed there for half an hour
I felt like I'd caught the flu

A chap passed I shouted, "Mate!
Is the 4:15 running late?"
"No trains run here, the line's too old
Your gonna catch your death of cold"

I thought I'd try and buy a gun
The bloke said, "'ave you got a license Son?"
"Can I have that gun on the shelf?"
"No chance lad you could kill yourself"

It's bloody hard work this suicide
I wanna take me final breath
I think the way I'm doomed to go
Is the wife nagging me to death.

THANK YOU LORD

My eight bedroom mansion is in its own grounds
I'm very happy here, it cost me 5 million pounds
I've got my own gardener, cook, chauffer as well
People see me and say he's done well I can tell

    I drive me Bentley on weekends
    Me Porsche through the week
    I check in my mirrors
    To make sure I look chic

I open my wallet full of credit cards and notes
It would choke a donkey if it got stuck in its throat

    My jewellery finishes my suaveness off well
    I'm good looking,
    I've got taste
    And I've got that expensive smell

    So when I say my prayers at night
    My very final thought
    Thank you Lord Almighty
    For inventing Income Support.

CHAIR

Nice to have that special chair
Rest your aching feet
A million thoughts in it everyday
As the world drifts down your street

It listens when you're laughing
Or having a little weep
It just sits there and holds you
When you need a little sleep

That chair knows all my secrets
They won't get spread about
Unlike telling your best friend
Who'll slowly leak them out

Worries seem to float away
Wave goodbye no time to stay
Used to think nobody cared
A problem told is a problem shared

So if you need a friendly ear
Believe me that time will come
I'll be alone here in my chair
I'll shove up half a bum.

THE GRAVEYARD

Took the wife to the cemetery today
She wanted to lay some flowers
I thought to myself, I'll keep her happy
It'll kill a couple of hours

There's nowt on the telly and I've read the paper
She'd already dragged me round town
It was a good idea, getting out for a drive
To visit old friends who are underground

Reading a few of the gravestones
Funny, I didn't remember them that way
But whenever they've passed over
It's strange what people say

I read me mate's wife's headstone
Says he worshipped her 'til the end
He must be getting her mixed up with someone else
'Cos she drove him round the bend

The next was Tom's girlfriends' headstone
Saying how loving and faithful she had been
Those words were very sincere and true
But it was to the local football team

We started counting all the graves
Of everyone we knew
She got up to 96
I got up to 92

Instead of feeling saddened
I started cheering up
She said, "What are you smiling for?"
I said, "Nothing butter-cup"

I started thinking of all my friends
Laying in their plots
And the money I'd have spent on birthday cards
Adds up to quite a lot

So coming out of the graveyard
Far from being depressed
All the money that I'm saving
I'm glad they're laid to rest.

MAN'S BEST FRIEND

Don't know how I'll get through today
Gonna lose my best friend
Gonna sit and hold his paw
Wanna be with him till the end

He keeps looking round at me
He knows there's summat up
The best mate I've ever had
Bought him as a pup

We've had our ups and downs
Looks like there'll be no more
On the bright side he'll miss Noel Edmonds tonight
He's getting put down at quarter to four

I like to think of his funny ways
How he'd always sit up and beg
Or when we'd watch Crufts together
He'd start and hump me leg

A wagging tail, a big wet nose
For anyone who calls
A kiss if you were unlucky
He'd usually been licking his balls

I'm gonna miss me doggy friends
And the bench where we used to sit
I'd have Fido close in one hand
And in the other me bag of shit

We're going on our last journey
A slow drive to the vet
Two hundred pounds for cremation
The bloody robbing git

I've loved our lives together
It's true man's best friend's a dog
Times like this I wish I'd bought a fish
I could've flushed him down the bog.

THIS IS ENGLAND

Evil nastiness in the school
Kids realise it's a handy tool
Bloody noses, splitting lips
Easy way to get on school trips

Soft teachers try to control
No hopers waiting for the dole
Killed a teacher, think it's funny?
Two weeks in Scarborough with spending money

Pensioners in by 7 o'clock
Bolt the door and double the lock
Too frightened to go out at night
Won the war but lost the fight

Druggies scurrying like little rats
Scrounging round like alley cats
Get their fix one way or another
Their needs too much, they'd rob their mother

Judges letting scum walk free
Barristers go for a bargain plea
Give him a chance to change his life
Would it be OK if he raped the Judge's wife?

'TWOCers' killing, dangerous driving
Killing outright, some surviving
Can't remember on drugs and pissed
You naughty boy 'ave a slap on the wrist

Burglars armed with a carving knife
Taking things you've worked for all your life
Breaking in, he knows you're on nights
You can't touch him he knows his rights

This is England what a tip
We hold our tongue and bite our lip
We won the war we should walk tall
In ten years time we'll own fuck all

DAD (Duggy Aged 10)

He's got his own smell me Dad
It isn't good and it isn't bad
I think it's how Dads must smell
What of? I couldn't tell

I like to watch telly sat on his knee
When there's only Dad and me
He lets me stay up when Mam's gone out
If it's after 8 my Mam would shout!

Dads face is always rough
He doesn't shave it close enough
His hands are huge and his nails are black
I love him to the moon and back

I dip me finger in his beer
He says, "That stuff gives you diarrhoea"
He might be joking, he might be right
But it keeps him up weeing half the night

I'm never frightened when I'm with Dad
Nowt could happen that was bad
I'm always safe holding my Dad's hand
He's the strongest man in all the land

I know me Dad has never cried
I know me Dad has never lied
He once fought a thousand men
Next day he fought them all again

He's good at football, good at darts
He's good at doing curly farts
He runs a mile in two minutes flat
Could any other Dad do that?

I like him to tuck me up in bed
He says, "Goodnight Son" and kisses me head
Too old for a story now I'm ten
But not too old for a cuddle now and again.

I squint my eyes up really tight
Won't come open 'til its light
Tell Jesus that I've been a good lad
Thank him for giving me my Dad

'AVEN'T THEY DONE WELL

Move away from Middlesbrough
Everyone's done well
They've found fame and fortune
If you believe the tales they tell

Our Michael, he's done well
A high flyer in the city
Married a nice cockney girl
Rich family and she's pretty

Our Ian, he's done marvellous
A police sergeant in Kent
He'll go straight to the top
('cos he's always been bent)

Our Sue, she works in Soho
She's found fortune and fame
She services the old men
She's spent years on the game

Our Sidney's down in Devon
Sells scones and cream teas
He works a 15 hour day
He's dead on his knees

Our Keith's in import/export
He's working abroad
He's in a Turkish jail

He got 10 years for fraud
Steven's done well
He's a gynaecologist in China
I suppose if you've seen one
Then you've seen every vagina

Quinten's a priest in the country
Peaceful, very little noise
Had me doubts about him
Over friendly with the altar boys

Our Andrea's done well in photography
She used to be a bit of a slag
Saw a part of her I'd never seen today
When I opened me porno mag

Our Robby's done so well
He's bought a huge villa in Spain
Lives with a lady boy
Likes gay sex and loves pain

Our Edward's in Australia
Passed as a vet, that's good news
Spends all of his days
Snipping balls off kangaroos

Moved away from Middlesbrough
They all got a better life
They're all on brilliant wages
They've all got a beautiful wife

They tell us all these stories
They're all driving HP cars
We just nod and listen
'Cos they're talking out their arse

WHO

Wouldn't it be lovely
As we knelt and said our prayers
God came and stood beside us
Like he'd just crept up the stairs

"I listen to you every night
I always hear you pray
You can have a loved one back
But only for the day"

Would you have your dad back?
You realise now he's dead
The things that he had done for you
Take back things you both said

Go and have a pint with him
You were always too busy lad
Say those words you were scared to say
"I don't half love yer Dad"

Or would you have yer mam back
To have those little walks
Try to solve your problems
When you had your little talks

She didn't always solve them
You'd get things off your chest
You were both too much alike
You both thought you knew best

Would you have your husband
Cuddle him once more
Tell him how much you're missing him
And how your heart is sore

Would you have your wife back
Kiss her smiling face
Say you're trying to move on
No one could take her place

Would you have your son back
Sit on the mat and play
Would it be too painful
To only have him for the day

Or have your little daughter
You called her your princess
Take her in town shopping
Buy her first new dress
Would you like your brother
To walk back through the door
You both fell out years ago
You both forgot what for

Would you love your sister
So alike in many ways
Have your nails and hair done
'Ave one of those girly days

Would you like your Nana
Wrinkly, old and wise
Ask her if you're doing things right
As she watches from the skies

Or would you 'ave your granddad
To tell you those tall tales
The tales kept getting taller
The more he sank Brown Ales

Would you love your dog back
Sit beside your feet
A roaring coal fire
As you watch Coronation Street

Would you like that special friend
On long cold winter nights
Have a drink together
And put the world to rights

Each night when I go to bed
I always say me prayers
For this story to come true
And God be at the top of the stairs.

Duggy's next book of poetry will be available in Spring 2012.

Keep in touch with Duggy at:
www.duggyverrill.com

Duggy recommends another book by an author from Middlesbrough, set in his home town.

'Out of Sync' by Scott Banner
available on Amazon